GUENTHER STEINER

A Detailed Biography

David Grey

TABLE OF CONTENTS

Have you ever watched a show or movie and found yourself really liking a character you didn't expect to? That's what happened with Guenther Steiner in the Formula One series, *Drive to Survive* on Netflix. He's a bit of a nerd who swears a lot and hasn't even seen the show before. But somehow, he's become really popular with viewers. It's weird because he's not even one of the famous drivers or their rich family members, or the head of the winning team. He's actually a middle-aged guy from Italy who manages a team of drivers that don't usually win.

His name is Guenther Steiner and he was born in 1965. He's a citizen of both Italy and the United States and used to work for other racing teams before becoming the leader of the Haas Formula One Team. Even though he's not a famous driver, people really like him and he's become a bit of a hero to some fans.

The Enthusiastic Engineer

Gunther Steiner grew up in Bolzano, Italy, where people speak German despite current boundaries linking it to Italy. Even though his dad was a butcher, Gunther wanted to be an engineer. He joined the military and then moved to Belgium in 1986 to work for the Mazda Rally Team Europe as a technician in the World Rally Championship. It was a watershed year for the Brussels, Belgium-based squad as they set to race the brand-new Mazda 323 four-wheel drive vehicle in Group A of the World Rally Championship after having previously competed in Group B with a Mazda RX-7. One of the two Group A Mazda 323s was assigned to Steiner and his crew of seven. In 1987,

Steiner and his crew were just in their second year of Group A competition when they guided Finnish driver Timo Salonen to victory in the season's second event, the Swedish Rally. With Salonen at the wheel, the team ended the season in sixth position in the Manufacturers World Championship standings and fourteenth in the Driver World Championship. After four years with Mazda Rally Team Europe, Salonen left the team in 1988 having earned fifth in the Driver World Championship and fourth in the Manufacturer World Championship.

In January of 1989, Gunther Steiner began his career at Top Run Srl as a mechanic. However, his exceptional skills and dedication quickly earned him a promotion to deputy team manager within a year. In this role, Steiner was responsible for overseeing the preparation and operation of private Group N rally vehicles for the Varese, Italy-based company.

During his time at Top Run Srl, Steiner and his crew worked tirelessly to coach Belgian driver Grégoire De Mévius to second place finishes in Group N of the World Rally Championships in both 1989 and 1990. The team achieved this impressive feat while driving a Mazda 323, a testament to Steiner's expertise and leadership.

In 1991 and 1992, Steiner joined Jolly Club Spa in Milan, Italy as the Group A team's head of reconnaissance. This move came after his success in the Group N division with Top Run Srl in the previous decade. At Jolly Club Spa, Steiner and his team raced Lancia Delta Integrale 16Vs in both seasons, contributing to Lancias victory in the Manufacturers World Championship.

In 1994, Steiner served as the technical coordinator for Jolly Club Spa's two Group A World Rally Championship Ford RS Cosworth teams. During the 1994 and 1995 seasons, Italian driver Gianfranco Cunico and his co-driver Stefano Evangelisti dominated the Italian Rally Championship, securing back-to-back victories. In 1996, Cunico teamed up with Pierangelo Scalvini to clinch the championship for a record-breaking third time.

In 1997, Steiner took on a new challenge as the manager of Prodrive's Allstar Rally Team, relocating to Banbury, Oxfordshire in the United Kingdom. With driver Krzysztof Holowczyc behind the wheel, Steiner led the rookie squad to victory in the European Championship in just their second year of competition.

After a year of working with Prodrive, Steiner was recruited by M-Sport in Millbrook, Bedfordshire, U.K. to oversee the Ford Focus cars in the World Rally Championship. In 1998, Ford had already commissioned M-Sport to create the chassis and body for the new Ford Focus World Rally Car, and Steiner was tasked with establishing the necessary infrastructure for developing the new automobile. With his expertise and leadership, Steiner quickly got to work and within eight months, he had moved into new offices and workshops, hired ten engineers and five technicians, and designed a whole new automobile - all under budget.

The new vehicle, driven by British driver Colin McRae, made its debut in the 1999 Monte Carlo Rally and quickly became the talk of the sport. M-Sport's triumph at the Safari Rally in Kenya marked their first World Rally Championship victory. McRae continued his winning streak, taking first place at the Rally of Portugal just a month later. Thanks to Steiner's guidance, the team achieved fourth place in the Manufacturers World Championship, while McRae placed sixth in the Drivers World Championship.

After leading M-Sport to victory in the 1999 World Rally Championship, Steiner was promoted to the position of Director of Engineering. As team leader, he took on more responsibility and relocated to a new headquarters to better coordinate the efforts of the many technical personnel involved in creating the Ford Focus World Rally Car.

In 2000, Steiner collaborated with legendary drivers Colin McRae and Carlos Sainz to secure second place in the Manufacturer World

Championship. Sainz placed third in the Driver World Championship, while McRae finished fourth. The following year, Steiner and his M-Sport Ford Focus teams once again secured second place in the Manufacturer World Championship. McRae narrowly missed out on the Driver World Championship, finishing just two points behind fellow British driver Richard Burns. Sainz, unfortunately, finished in last place, 11 points behind Burns.

Steiner's leadership and technical expertise were instrumental in the success of M-Sport during this period. His ability to coordinate the efforts of a large team of technical personnel was crucial in the development of the Ford Focus World Rally Car. Despite narrowly missing out on the top spot in the Manufacturer World Championship, Steiner and his team can be proud of their impressive achievements during this time.

In 2001, Niki Lauda, the Formula One champion, recognized the administrative and technical expertise of Steiner and invited him to join Jaguar Racing as the team's managing director. Steiner accepted the offer and was appointed on December 3rd. He was responsible for overseeing the engineering department in Milton Keynes, while John Allison, the director of strategy, managed the business operations.

Steiner wasted no time in reorganizing the club and making necessary adjustments to the budget and staff in preparation for the 2002 season. Despite his efforts, Jaguar struggled that year, with Eddie Irvine scoring only eight championship points and Pedro de la Rosa failing to score at all. As a result,

Ford, the parent company of Jaguar, fired Lauda on November 26 and laid off 70 team personnel.

After the 2002 season, Steiner decided to take a break from the fast-paced world of racing and embark on a gardening vacation. This decision came after a management shakeup at Jaguar Racing, which resulted in Steiner being succeeded by project manager David Pitchforth. Despite being offered another position on the team, Steiner declined and instead began working at the Opel Performance Center in Bobingen, Germany in November of 2003.

At Opel, Steiner quickly rose through the ranks and took over as technical director after the departure of Wiet Huidekoper. In this role, he oversaw the company's technical and production operations and spearheaded a technical restructuring to facilitate future growth. As the head of the team's group of engineers, Steiner was intimately involved in the day-to-day operations of the company and was often found near the track, ensuring that everything was running smoothly.

Rise to Prominence in Motorsports

In February of 2005, Gunther Steiner joined Red Bull Racing as the technical operations chief. This move came after Red Bull acquired Jaguar Racing in November of 2004. Steiner's decision to rejoin the Milton Keynes squad was prompted by Opel's decision to leave the Deutsche Tourenwagen Masters at the end of 2005. On January 13, 2005, he was officially approved for the position of technical operations director.

Steiner was placed back in control of the reorganization he had begun in 2001 until 2003. His extensive background in team management was put to the test once again when he oversaw the Formula One team's technical operations. With over 350 workers and a budget of over $200 million, Steiner had his work cut out for him.

In 2005, the team's fortunes improved under Steiner and team principal Christian Horner. However, after Red Bull hired McLaren's championship-winning technical director Adrian Newey, McLaren owner Dietrich Mateschitz asked Steiner to help found a NASCAR team in North Carolina.

After consulting with his wife, Steiner decided to relocate to Mooresville, North Carolina on April 2006, to serve as Team Red Bull's technical director until April 2008. This was a challenging time for Steiner, but he rose to the occasion and helped establish the team as a force to be reckoned with in NASCAR.

Steiner's ability to build a championship-caliber team from scratch is truly remarkable. He seized yet another opportunity to do so by relocating to the United States. In April of 2006, Steiner embarked on this journey with nothing but a blank slate, no workers, and no equipment. Fast forward to today, and Team Red Bull boasts a team of over 200 employees and a budget exceeding $50 million. Steiner's vision and leadership have been instrumental in the success of Team Red Bull. Their dedication to excellence and commitment to innovation make them a force to be reckoned with in the world of motorsports.

The Story behind Haas

In April 2008, Guenther Steiner parted ways with Team Red Bull, but he remained in Mooresville. However, in January 2009, he founded FibreWorks Composites, a company that specialized in designing and producing high-tech carbon composites for racing vehicles.

Fast forward to April 14th, 2014, and Steiner was introduced to the world as the new team principal for Haas F1. But before Haas F1 was established, there were a series of setbacks for an existing F1 team. The foundation of Haas was laid as a result of an unsuccessful American initiative-The US F1. In 2009, the US F1 Team approached Steiner about working with them towards their 2010 debut. Steiner had a deep desire to be part of the sport again at the highest levels, and this opportunity seemed like the perfect fit.

***

The United States Formula One Team was granted entry into the highly competitive 2010 Formula One season. However, to the disappointment of many fans, the team failed to participate in any races that year. As a result, the FIA was forced to remove them from the list of entrants.

The team was led by two highly respected individuals in the racing world: Ken Anderson, a former technical director for Haas CNC Racing, and Peter Windsor, a journalist and former manager for Williams and Ferrari. Their goal was to establish the first F1 team outside of Europe, with their headquarters located in Charlotte, North Carolina.

One of the team's most ambitious plans was to feature two American drivers in the 2010 season. This was a bold move aimed at showcasing American talent and innovation in the racing world. Unfortunately, the team was unable to compete, leaving fans and supporters disappointed.

It all started on February 24, 2009, when Peter Windsor and Ken Anderson made a groundbreaking announcement on the American cable television network Speed Channel. They revealed their plans to enter a new Formula One team, US F1, for the 2010 Formula One World Championship. This was a significant moment for American motorsport, as it marked the first time in over a decade that the United States would have a team competing in the prestigious event.

After months of anticipation, the United States Formula One Team was officially admitted to the 2010 Formula One World Championship on June 12, 2009. However, the road to success was not without its challenges. The political dispute between the FIA and FOTA in the summer of 2009 caused delays in the signing of the Concorde Agreement between US F1 and the FIA. It wasn't until July 29, 2009, that the final agreements were signed, and some budgetary restrictions and technical rules that had been up for negotiation were lifted.

Unfortunately, these delays had a knock-on effect on the manufacturing timetable, causing further setbacks for the team

In mid-February, the American Formula One team was facing financial difficulties that threatened to force them to fold. In an effort to salvage their season, the team requested to start the season with the Spanish Grand Prix instead of the first four races. However, senior staff members criticized Peter Windsor and Ken Anderson for mismanagement, which had slowed down the design and construction processes. As a result, the FIA began considering alternatives.

On February 24, 2010, the FIA conducted a readiness inspection of the team's facilities. One week later, it was announced that the United States Formula One team was not competitive. A potential merger between Stefan Grand Prix and US F1 was explored but ultimately failed. Anderson and Hurley requested to postpone their entrance until 2011, but the FIA reopened registration entirely.

Unfortunately, the team was unable to recover from their financial struggles and was forced to

disband forever. On March 2, the entire team was let go, and by March 3, the FIA had already altered its entry list to exclude American F1.
To satisfy a creditor, the crew had to sell their trailers on eBay.

The FIA penalized the American Formula One team €309,000 on June 24 and disqualified them from all FIA-sanctioned races for the rest of the season. It was a devastating blow for the team and a reminder of the harsh realities of the sport. Despite their best efforts, the American Formula One team was unable to overcome the financial and economic difficulties that ultimately led to their downfall.

However, Steiner's journey to becoming a Formula 1 team principal was not without its challenges. It all began when his firm was tasked with doing some work for the US F1 team, and he was formally introduced to their team principal, Ken Anderson. Steiner was immediately drawn to the project and proceeded to devote himself fully to it after making contact with the financier, Chad Hurley.

However, Stefano Domenicali, the previous manager of the Ferrari team, saw that working with Hurley was not going anywhere and suggested that Steiner abandon the project. Stefano's prediction proved to be correct, as the US F1 team disbanded shortly afterward and never raced again. But Steiner was undeterred; he had been considering starting his own Formula 1 team for some time.

After the FIA lifted its restriction on ordering a vehicle from a known builder, Steiner began approaching potential backers. One of them was

Gene Haas, a NASCAR teams founder. Steiner went to great lengths to connect with individuals in the racing industry who knew Haas, even treating them to steak dinners. Eventually, Haas was persuaded and sought help obtaining a license. He also brought in 10-time podium finisher Romain Grosjean to be the team's driver leader.

Despite the challenges and setbacks, Steiner's determination and persistence paid off.

Steiner's extensive background in racing made him the perfect candidate to start a new Formula One team from scratch. As the team principal, he was responsible for recruiting and hiring a top-tier team of engineers, technicians, and drivers. According to Autosport, Steiner is the driving force behind the team, responsible for hiring core members, conducting interviews with potential team members, and forming strategic alliances with suppliers Dallara and Ferrari.

The Haas F1 Team's partnership with Ferrari has been one of its most distinguishing features since its inception. In fact, the 2016 season marked the first time in over 30 years that a team used engines and technical assistance from a team other than their own manufacturer. This partnership has been crucial to the team's success, allowing them to draw on the knowledge and facilities of one of the most dominant forces in Formula One.

However, Steiner knew that building a winning Formula One team required more than just technical know-how. He understood that he needed to foster an environment where employees valued invention, creativity, and cooperation above all else. This meant finding individuals who believed in his mission and were willing to put in long hours to see it through.

Steiner and his team dedicated countless hours to transforming Haas F1 into a formidable contender in the world of Formula One. Despite facing numerous obstacles, including regulatory roadblocks, budgetary constraints, and fierce competition from seasoned teams, Steiner remained steadfast in his ultimate goal of assembling a championship-caliber squad. He challenged Haas engineers to create cutting-edge innovations that would set the company apart from its rivals.

In 2016, Haas became the first American constructor to enter Formula One in 30 years, with Gene Haas, the creator of CNC machine tool firm Haas Automation, at the helm. Although the team did not have an American driver, the arrival of

Romain Grosjean and Esteban Gutierrez was highly anticipated. The VF-16, the team's first vehicle, performed exceptionally well in preseason testing, raising hopes for the season opener.

Despite early difficulties in qualifying, both Grosjean and Gutierrez performed admirably in the race, earning praise for the team's inaugural performance as one of the best in recent Formula One history.

The Haas F1 Team had an impressive start to the season, culminating in a triumphant performance at the Bahrain Grand Prix. Romain Grosjean's fifth-place finish marked the team's first points in only their second race and was seen as a pivotal moment for the club, signaling the beginning of a fruitful season.

Following a promising debut season, the Haas F1 Team was poised for continued success in the world of Formula One. With Grosjean's impressive points haul, the team earned a total of 29, placing them seventh in the constructor standings - the highest of any new team at the time. With a strong start to the season, the team had firmly established itself as a serious contender in the sport.

In 2017, Kevin Magnussen replaced Gutiérrez as the teammate of Grosjean in the Haas Formula One team. The season opener saw Grosjean qualify the VF-17 in sixth position, which was the best result in the car's history. Unfortunately, both vehicles had to withdraw from the race due to technical issues. However, Magnussen managed to secure eighth place in the second race weekend, earning his first point since the 2016 Singapore

Grand Prix. Haas also scored their first point since the 2016 United States Grand Prix when Grosjean finished in tenth place.

Haas continued to impress in Monaco, with Grosjean finishing in eighth place and Magnussen in tenth. The team went on to achieve their first-ever double-point finish in the same race later that year. Despite being overtaken by the Renault Sport Formula One Team in the last few races, Haas managed to secure eighth place in the constructors' championship.

Overall, the 2017 season was a mixed bag for Haas, with some impressive performances and some technical issues.

Several of Haas' competitors demanded an inquiry after the company unveiled their new VF-18 supercar in February 2018, claiming that it bore too much resemblance to Ferrari's SF70H from the previous year. Despite the controversy, Haas maintained their competitive edge from winter testing into the Australian Grand Prix weekend, with Kevin Magnussen qualifying in fifth and Romain Grosjean in sixth. However, both cars crashed one lap after their respective pit stops while in fourth and fifth place, respectively, which would have been their best finish and half of their 2017-point total.

Notwithstanding the setback, Haas went on to achieve their greatest year yet in 2018, placing fifth in the Constructors Championship and coming within one point of matching their performance from the previous year. In fact, they set a new company record in the Singapore Grand Prix when Magnussen set Haas' quickest lap ever. The team's success was evident in their collection of 93 points, making the 2018 season their best in Formula One.

In 2019, the Haas F1 Team proudly announced Rich Energy as its title sponsor. The British energy drink manufacturer, which had previously been linked to a purchase of Force India, activated its multiyear title sponsorship agreement with the Indian racing team at this time. The team retained its driver pairing of Grosjean and Magnussen from the previous year, and their car for the season was the VF-19.

Despite the VF-19's impressive qualifying times, the car struggled to maintain its speed during actual races. Magnussen's sixth-place finish in the season-opening race in Australia was the team's best performance of the year. In Austria, the team's qualifying speed was on full display as Magnussen set the fifth-fastest time, but both he and Grosjean finished well outside the top ten.

The team's poor performance was cited in a tweet from the Rich Energy Twitter account, announcing the termination of the sponsorship deal just four days before the British Grand Prix in July. However, the team and Rich Energy's stockholders disputed this, attributing the tweet to a rogue employee.

In an effort to figure out what went wrong with the car in Australia and how to fix it for the next race, the team decided to run Grosjean's vehicle to the same standard as in Australia at the British Grand Prix. Unfortunately, on the very first lap, both drivers were involved in an accident that forced them to withdraw.

The team's best finish of the year came in the German Grand Prix, where they finished seventh and eighth overall after post-race penalties were handed out to other drivers. Despite the challenges faced throughout the season, the Haas F1 Team remained committed to improving and pushing forward.

The primary sponsor, Rich Energy, faced a tumultuous year in court, facing allegations of copying another company's logo (Whyte Bikes) among other issues. Following the Italian Grand Prix in September, Rich Energy publicly announced the termination of its contract with Haas. Unfortunately, the team's performance at Monza was lackluster, with Grosjean finishing in 16th place and Magnussen retiring, resulting in zero points for the team.

Haas' final score of 28 points was the lowest the team has achieved in the Constructors Championship since its establishment in 2016.

Haas maintained their 2020 lineup with Grosjean and Magnussen, hoping to improve on their previous year's performance. While Magnussen finished ninth in Hungary, a time penalty dropped him to tenth, and Grosjean finished ninth in the Eifel Grand Prix, earning Haas three points in the 2020 Formula One World Championship. Unfortunately, the team was unable to score again, resulting in their lowest point total in history and a ninth-place finish in the constructors championship.

The Bahrain Grand Prix proved to be a turning point for the team, as Grosjean was involved in a horrific accident with Daniil Kvyat of AlphaTauri. The collision sent both drivers crashing over the barriers between Turns 3 and 4, with Grosjean's car smashed in two and catching fire. Despite suffering burns to his hands, Grosjean narrowly avoided serious harm, thanks in part to the halo helmet shield. Haas replaced him with backup driver Pietro Fittipaldi for the Sakhir Grand Prix the following week.

At the end of the 2020 season, Grosjean departed from Haas after a year of tension with team principal Guenther Steiner. Despite their disagreements, Steiner acknowledged Grosjean's value to the team, having scored 104 points since joining Haas. While Grosjean never led the team to the podium, his efforts were still considered impressive by the team.

In the 2021 season, Kevin Magnussen remained with the club but took on the roles of test and reserve driver. He was replaced by Nikita Mazepin of Russia and Mick Schumacher, the 2020 Formula 2 champion and son of seven-time F1 world champion Michael Schumacher. However, the team made the decision to halt work on the 2021 automobile to save funds for the 2022 project.

Uralkali, a Russian potash fertilizer firm in which Mazepin's father, Dmitry, who has a significant stake, agreed to be the team's headline sponsor. As a result of Uralkali's support, the team's livery features the national colors of Russia. Some have disputed that this was done to circumvent a prohibition on the Russian flag by the World Anti-Doping Agency, but team principal Guenther Steiner had denied these claims.

Unfortunately, Mazepin's debut was short-lived as he crashed out on the first lap, and Schumacher finished 16th. Mazepin also tested positive for coronavirus and was disqualified from the last race of the season. As a result, the team decided to field just one driver instead of having Magnussen replace Mazepin, as Magnussen had not yet participated in a practice session.

Following Russia's annexation of Ukraine, Haas removed the Uralkali logo and Russian flag colors from their automobiles. The team's championship sponsorship agreement with Uralkali and the driver contract with Mazepin were officially terminated on March 5th. Unfortunately, Haas was unable to inform Nikita in person due to a breakdown in communication with the Mazepin father-son duo. Nine days after the siege began, Mazepin Jr. learned of the news through the media and expressed his frustration with the team. The Mazepins and Haas parted ways on a sour note. Nikita filed a lawsuit against the team for allegedly underpaying him, but Steiner claims they had a private conversation beforehand, which Nikita strongly denies.

Despite the setback, Steiner led the team's return in 2022 with renewed hope and determination. The VF-21 went through the entire previous season without any upgrades or modifications, as resources were being diverted to the team's replacement. Haas brought back veteran Kevin Magnussen after a late driver change and the dissolution of the previous title sponsor, giving the team a fresh start for the longest season in Formula 1 history.

Haas made a bold move by dedicating the entirety of the 2021 season to developing their VF-22 vehicle. This decision paid off as they were able to field a competitive car that could keep up with the rest of the pack. The team's fortunes were boosted by the return of Kevin Magnussen, who helped Haas score points in the first two races of the season in Bahrain and Saudi Arabia. However, Mick Schumacher, despite his strong qualifying positions, failed to earn any points in either race. In fact, he didn't even make the starting lineup in Saudi Arabia after crashing out in qualifying.

Despite their initial success, Haas faced challenges in subsequent races due to frequent collisions with other cars. This made it difficult for both Magnussen and Schumacher to score points and finish races.

In the 2022 British Grand Prix, Haas Racing Team's Kevin Magnussen finished in 10th place, while Michael Schumacher secured the 8th position. This marked a significant milestone for the team, as it was their first double-point finish in three years, and Magnussen's first point finish in Formula One. The momentum continued in the 2022 Austrian Grand Prix, with Magnussen finishing in 8th place and Schumacher in 6th, showcasing the team's consistency and determination.

Following the Hungarian Grand Prix, Haas Racing Team's back-to-back double-point finishes propelled them to the 7th position in the Constructors Championship. This impressive feat was made possible by the team's acquisition of a superior Ferrari engine, which has been the envy of the sport. The team's success did not go unnoticed, with many referring to them as the "white Ferrari."

However, team principal Guenther Steiner ha been quick to defend his squad against claims of a recent uptick in performance. He attributes their success to the team's tireless efforts and dedication, rather than simply relying on their engine.

Magnussen emerged victorious at the Grand Prix of Sao Paulo, triumphing over a fiercely competitive field in a qualifying session that was plagued by unpredictable conditions. This remarkable achievement marked the team's first pole position, a momentous occasion that was celebrated by all. However, the race itself was not without its challenges, as Magnussen was involved in a collision with McLaren's Daniel Ricciardo early on, which ultimately forced him to withdraw from the race.

In other news, it was announced that Schumacher would be departing from Haas at the end of the season. This decision was met with mixed reactions, as Schumacher had been a valued member of the team for many years.

Starting in the 2023 season and beyond, MoneyGram will be the primary sponsor of the Haas F1 Team. An official agreement has been launched between the MoneyGram Haas F1 Team and Chipotle Mexican Grill in anticipation of the 2023 FIA Formula 1 World Championship. This exciting partnership means that MoneyGram Haas F1 Team drivers Kevin Magnussen and Nico Hulkenberg, as well as team equipment, will proudly display the Chipotle Mexican Grill emblem on the nose and side of the VF-23.

Prior to the 2022 Abu Dhabi Grand Prix, it was announced that Nico Hulkenberg would be returning to Formula One for the 2023 season as Magnussen's teammate. Haas confirmed early in

2023 that Pietro Fittipaldi would continue to serve as the team's official test and reserve driver. Fittipaldi, a two-time Grand Prix starter, will spend his sixth straight season assisting the sole American team in the FIA Formula 1 World Championship and developing the VF-23. After testing the VF-18 and VF-19, Fittipaldi jumped into the cockpit of the VF-20 to replace an injured Romain Grosjean for the last two rounds of the 2020 FIA Formula 1 World Championship.

This exciting news is a testament to the Haas F1 Team's commitment to excellence and their dedication to building strong partnerships with leading companies like MoneyGram and Chipotle Mexican Grill. With Hulkenberg's return and Fittipaldi's continued involvement, the team is poised for success in the upcoming season and beyond. Fans can look forward to seeing the iconic

Chipotle Mexican Grill emblem on the VF-23 as the MoneyGram Haas F1 Team takes to the track in pursuit of victory.

Growing? or racing in circles?

The Haas F1 Team has made a name for itself in the world of Formula One, amassing an impressive 70 top-ten finishes throughout its career. In 2018, the team had its finest year yet, placing fifth in the Constructors Championship and securing 22 top-ten finishes. Despite this success, the team has yet to claim a victory in Formula One. However, the team's early seasons showed great promise, with a strong start in their debut season and multiple top-ten finishes in subsequent years.

While the Haas F1 Team has faced its fair share of challenges since joining Formula One in 2016, it has always taken a unique approach to the sport. Owner Gene Haas broke into Formula One with a budget strategy that allowed newer, smaller teams to compete. While this approach has allowed the team to remain competitive despite its limited budget, it has also had an impact on the team's overall success. In fact, in 2020, Haas reportedly questioned whether investing tens of millions in the team was worth it after a disappointing ninth-place finish in the constructors' championship.

Over the years, the Haas F1 team has undergone several changes in its driver roster. From Romain Grosjean to Kevin Magnussen, Nikita Mazepin, and Mick Schumacher, the team has given many drivers a chance to prove their mettle. However, these alterations have not always resulted in better outcomes. After a disappointing 2020 season, the team decided to substitute Grosjean and Magnussen with two rookies, and surprisingly, they enhanced their 2023 driver roster even more.

Many people hoped that the team's decision would provide Mick Schumacher, the son of seven-time Formula One world winner Michael Schumacher, with a second chance. However, the team management made the tough decision to break ways with Schumi and replace him with Nico Hulkenberg, a fellow German who is 11 years older than the youthful driver. Schumacher's crashes in 2022 severely damaged Haas' chances of re-signing him for the following season.

Despite operating on a tiny budget, the team has remained competitive. However, signing a top-tier driver like Lewis Hamilton, Fernando Alonso, or the current world champion, Max Verstappen, will be a hard task. Nevertheless, the squad remains dedicated to the game and will continue to train to become better.

The Haas F1 Team has always been committed to constant growth and evolution, and this drive will continue into the 2023 season. Team principal Guenther Steiner has expressed his excitement for the future of the organization, highlighting the team's positive growth in 2023. One area the team is focusing on this season is improving their pit stop performance.

The Haas F1 Team has been working hard both on and off the track to become a more formidable squad. Recent changes in the team's driver lineup have helped in this endeavor, with the addition of fresh talent aimed at improving performance. With seven points, the team is currently in seventh place out of 10 teams, with Alpine leading McLaren by one point.

For the 2023 season, the team has revealed a new look to coincide with their new multi-year championship relationship with MoneyGram. The club's new livery reflects this exciting partnership. Additionally, the team is aiming for a more consistent duo of drivers with the addition of German star Nico Hulkenberg to the roster alongside Kevin Magnussen.

It would be unwise to underestimate Haas' chances of challenging for the fifth spot following Red Bull, Aston Martin, Mercedes-AMG, and Ferrari if Hulkenberg can shake off the rest of his racing rust and Magnussen picks up the pace. The team is determined to continue its upward trajectory and make its mark in the world of F1.

The Netflix Star

Before the release of the Netflix series *Drive to Survive* in 2018, Guenther Steiner was not a well-known figure, even among casual fans of the sport.

The documentary style of Netflix was perfect for building Steiner's profile. Instead of providing a chronological rundown of an F1 season, the program focused on a single story at a time. It was during this time that they realized Steiner had star potential.

Haas and the other teams on the grid received greater coverage since Ferrari and Mercedes did not participate in the inaugural season. Steiner quickly became the brightest star in the spotlight. His unvarnished thoughts were accepted by fans all around the globe, and he rapidly became a fan favorite.

As a result of Steiner's newfound fame, Formula 1 experienced a dramatic increase in web views, ticket sales, and F1TV subscriptions beginning with the first season of Drive to Survive.

In 2022, at the bustling Mexico City airport, a young girl of around 16 years old was in such a hurry to get a signature or photo from a certain someone that she ended up falling flat on her face on the smooth, hard floor. Guenther, the Haas team principal, didn't witness the collision, but he was aware of the growing crowd around him. In an effort to avoid drawing attention to himself, he quickly switched places in line.

Guenther Steiner, the breakout star of the film, has gained notoriety for his candid and, let's be honest, expletive-laden way of speaking. As a result, he is constantly in the public eye no matter where he goes. Since his first appearance in 2018, Steiner has been a regular on the program, providing viewers with countless memorable moments and remarks. His interactions with all of his drivers, from Romain Grosjean and Nikita Mazepin to Kevin Magnussen and beyond, have been nothing short of amusing.

In the latest season, the fifth installment, an episode is dedicated to the tumultuous relationship between Italian-American Steiner and American owner Gene Haas. The episode centers around the firing of Mick Schumacher, despite his legendary last name, due to his lack of skill on the track. The cameras capture Steiner's frustration as he confronts the team for letting Mick down, calling him a "dead man walking" and hurling other insults.

The episode paints a vivid picture of Schumacher's struggles as a rookie driver, and the tension between him and Steiner is palpable. However, despite their differences, Steiner was quick to dismiss any claims of harassment towards Mick. He explained that his harsh assessment was made in the heat of the moment and that his more moderate opinions of Schumacher's abilities were likely left on the cutting room floor.

It's clear that Steiner and Schumacher's relationship was strained, but the episode sheds light on the difficult decisions that team bosses must make in the competitive world of Formula One. Ultimately, Schumacher was replaced by the more skilled and competent Nico Hulkenberg for the current season.

In March of 2023, Guenther Steiner made his way into the FOX broadcast booth to provide expert analysis of the NASCAR Cup Series race at COTA (Circuit of the Americas). Steiner's unexpected rise to worldwide fame, thanks to the Netflix series *Drive to Survive,* has made him a household name in the United States as well.

Despite his newfound celebrity status, Steiner insists that he has never watched an episode of the show. He believes that this allows him to remain true to himself and not alter his actions for the sake of the camera. His wife Gertraud, on the other hand, is an avid viewer, but his 13-year-old daughter is not allowed to watch due to her father's colorful language.

Steiner's unique accent, which is a blend of German, Italian, and American, has endeared him to fans of the sport. They appreciate his no-nonsense attitude and his willingness to speak his mind, even if it means using a few choice expletives to describe the challenges of managing a lower-ranking team.

Achievements

Mr. Steiner has an impressive career in the motorsports industry. He began as a mechanic for Mazda Rally Team Europe and later served as an assistant team manager for Top Run Srl in the FIA World Rally Championship. He then moved on to become the head of reconnaissance for Jolly Club Spa and later served as the technical manager for the same team in Italy. Mr. Steiner's career continued to flourish as he joined Prodrive as the team manager for its Allstar Rally Team. He then became the project manager for M-Sport and led the team's Ford Focus fleet to a fourth-place finish in the manufacturer standings of the FIA World Rally Championship. He also served as a director of engineering for M-Sport and worked with legendary drivers such as McRae and Sainz. Under Mr. Steiner's leadership, M-Sport achieved a second straight runner-up finish in the manufacturer standings of the FIA World Rally Championship. He was then named managing director for Jaguar Racing in the FIA Formula One World Championship. After that, he joined Opel Performance Center as a technical director and developed a brand-new U.S. Formula 1 Team with Gene Haas. Mr. Steiner's expertise in the industry led him to be named technical operations director for Red Bull Racing in the FIA Formula One World Championships. He also set up Red Bull Racing in the NASCAR Sprint Cup Series. Finally, he founded FibreWorks Composites in North Carolina and is currently holding a significant position in Haas F1.

The Steiners

Steiner, along with his wife Gertraud and their daughter, are proud dual citizens of both the United States and Italy. They have made their home in the charming town of Mooresville, North Carolina. Gertraud is a stunning woman with gorgeous long hair and a charming grin that lights up any room she enters.

Recently, Gertraud made an appearance on the new series *Drive to Survive,* where the camera followed her and her husband to their house in Merano, Italy. The Steiners have been happily married for years, and they are the proud parents of a little girl named Greta Steiner.

Gertraud takes great pleasure in tweeting photos of the couple together at all the many events they attend, as well as birthday greetings to her beloved husband. She has also taken to her role as a racing engineer's wife, touring with him around the country. However, her most important role is that of a mother, which she takes great pride in.

Their daughter, Greta, has a passion for watercolor painting, which Gertraud often shares on her Twitter account. The family's trilingualism is thanks to Steiner's upbringing in South Tyrol, where he learned German, Italian, and English.

Summary

Born in Italy to a German family, Steiner always had a knack for engineering and mechanics. After working his way through the ranks at various European racing teams, Steiner made his mark as an integral part of Jaguar Racing's technical staff during their 2004 season. From there, he went on to work with Williams and Red Bull before landing himself a position as team principal at Haas F1 Team – where he currently resides. Known for his no-nonsense approach and sharp wit, Steiner has become a cult figure among fans due to his memorable radio exchanges and on-track meltdowns.

Guenther Steiner, the Haas team manager, tied the knot with Gertraud Steiner and welcomed their daughter, Greta Steiner, into the world. However, Steiner's latest achievement is his upcoming book, *Surviving to Drive*, set to be published in April 2023. This will be his first work of nonfiction, and it has already been picked up by Transworld Publishers, a division of the Penguin Random House media company, for publication in the United Kingdom and the Commonwealth.

Surviving to Drive is a journal that Steiner kept during the 2022 Formula 1 season, providing readers with an inside look into the Haas team's journey. The book takes readers on an emotional roller coaster, showcasing the highs and lows of life in the sports highest stakes arena. Steiner discusses how being a racing manager is far more demanding than managing a football team, and readers will gain a newfound appreciation for the complexities of the sport.

The 2022 Formula 1 season saw both Kevin Magnussen and Mick Schumacher score points for Haas, with Magnussen picking up some eye-catching successes early in the year. *Surviving to Drive* will delve into the team's experiences throughout the season, revealing what goes on behind the scenes in the management of a Formula 1 team.

Steiner is thrilled to be publishing his first book. *Surviving to Drive* promises to be an exciting and insightful read for anyone interested in the world of Formula 1.

Given his meteoric climb to fame since his initial appearance on the Netflix program Drive to Survive, Steiner's decision to publish a book may come as no great surprise.

With his straightforward and profanity-laced approach to being an F1 team boss, he has gained a legion of admirers throughout the show's four seasons. It's no wonder that the title of his upcoming book pays homage to the impact the Netflix series has had on his life. Transworld is set to release the book in April 2023, and fans are eagerly anticipating a deeper understanding of this eccentric team leader's personality in the world of Formula One.

With plenty more years left in the sport, we can only hope that Guenther continues to bring his unique blend of brilliance and humor to Formula One.